THE YOUNG MOGULS

Empower Your Business, Embrace Your Hustle

SHAWN SMALLS

TABLE OF CONTENTS

DEDICATION V

ACKNOWLEDGMENT VII

CHAPTER 1
THE POTENTIAL ENTREPRENEUR 1

CHAPTER 2
ENTREPRENEUR VS. EMPLOYEE 5

CHAPTER 3
CHARACTERISTICS OF THE SUCCESSFUL
ENTREPRENEUR 9

CHAPTER 4
BUSINESS BLUEPRINT 13

CHAPTER 5
ENTREPRENEURIAL ASSESSMENT 21

CHAPTER 6
BUSINESS IDEA 27

CHAPTER 7
LEGAL REQUIREMENTS 31

CHAPTER 8
RECORD KEEPING 35

CHAPTER 9
BUSINESS STRUCTURE 41

CHAPTER 10
CUSTOMER SERVICE 47

CHAPTER 11
SELLING 53

CHAPTER 12
BUSINESS PLAN 59

CHAPTER 13
THE MARKETING MIX 65

CHAPTER 14
COMPETITION 69

DEDICATION

This book is dedicated to the multitude of children whom I've had the honor to guide nationwide on the path towards economic independence and entrepreneurship. The journey has been a shared one, with both A.C.E. Academy Charter School and the Young Moguls program. Both creations sparked from the passion that was kindled in me during my own childhood. These programs have been instrumental in shaping the future entrepreneurs of our society. The gratitude I have for your role in bringing my vision to life is immense. Your role has been integral in my mission to revolutionize the way our community's approach financial education and entrepreneurship.

ACKNOWLEDGMENT

In the depths of my heart, there's an ocean of gratitude for you, Laila, my life's love. Our paths crossed not by accident but by the meaningful intention of the universe. You've been my wind, lifting me, aiding me in soaring high, just as the wind does to a bird. Your devotion and love for our family is a treasure beyond measure. To my precious daughters, Jordan and Jewel, your very existence is a spark that lights my soul, helping me overcome life's hurdles. You are the embodiment of love in my life, a role you will forever hold. SJ, my son, your hunger for success inspires me to keep my focus, continually pushing for personal and professional growth. Watching you evolve into a remarkable entrepreneur, ready to take up my legacy, is an honor beyond words. To my dear family, your presence is the driving force behind my aspirations. You are my "WHY," the center of my universe, and my love for you is limitless.

Loving you always,

Dad

CHAPTER 1
THE POTENTIAL ENTREPRENEUR

Do you want to start a business but aren't sure if you have the right skills or have the pedigree? Before you tackle such a venture, it will be wise to ask yourself, what will it take to become an entrepreneur as you run through so many obstacles and challenges? As you develop your entrepreneurial character traits, you will need to understand what your strengths and weaknesses are as you navigate through the business maze. Entering the unknown battlefield of business can be very scary for anyone because of the high risk it will take to succeed.

Remember to write down your business goals and analyze how you will achieve them in pursuing your ultimate dream of business ownership.

As you develop your skills to become this fascinating entrepreneur, you will have many obstacles in your way including family and friends who might not understand the fire you have in your heart to create this business. Always remember:

- Opportunity doesn't wait for anyone
- Do thorough research in the business you want to start
- Be persistent and go super hard
- Have a team player mentality
- Be customer driven
- Have a positive attitude
- Have fun while you are building your empire

Life Begins at the End of Your Comfort Zone

Over half of the workforce in the United States is created by small businesses. As innovation develops, more jobs are being created to keep up with the demand and technology. The youth is leading the way to this innovation as they are using social media platforms to sell their ideas and create new ways to do business. Creating a wonderful opportunity for the youth to see their true potential as they navigate through the business world preparing for a journey that will bring a variety of experiences that will last a lifetime.

This book is your starter kit to get you going in helping you become interested in business. Kids from elementary to college can take advantage of the knowledge being shared in this book. You need to strap in to get your grind on and run this marathon called business ownership.

CHAPTER 2
ENTREPRENEUR VS. EMPLOYEE

An employee is someone who earns a living by working for someone else. An entrepreneur is both owner and employee. An entrepreneur assumes risk and is responsible for the success or failure of his or her business. If being independent, working long hours, taking risks and potentially amassing wealth are your goals, then entrepreneurship is right for you.

Here are some differences between an entrepreneur and an employee:

Entrepreneur Attributes

- An entrepreneur values freedom over job security.
- An entrepreneur does not accept limits on how much money they can make.
- Builds financial security.
- Builds his or her assets.
- Can make money at the business location or sitting at home.
- An entrepreneur has the potential to make an infinite amount of money.

- Studies the market, target customers and competition before going into business.
- An entrepreneur is willing to take calculated and educated risks.
- Entrepreneurs build businesses with processes that benefit them.
- Pays taxes on net income.
- Entrepreneurs' income is taxed in a lower bracket.
- An entrepreneur chooses a business structure that provides the best limitation of liability and minimizes taxes.
- Can use all their business skills.

- Controls the direction the business will go.
- Will put together a business plan mapping out a route for success.

To become a successful entrepreneur, you must establish the right business mindset instead of thinking like an employee.

Employee Attributes

- Values job security over wealth.
- Doesn't have financial security.
- Works to build their employer's business or assets.
- Only make money if they are working.
- Income is taxed at the highest bracket.
- Employees are paid for time and the average are paid for only 20% of what they are worth to the business.
- Only uses a small percentage of their skills.
- Pays taxes on total income.
- Usually doesn't control the direction of the business.
- Build business processes that benefit their employer.

The greatest thing about being an entrepreneur or an employee is you get to choose the direction you want to go. Some people start off being an employee then decide to open their dream business. There isn't a right or wrong choice, but if you like excitement and challenges then being an entrepreneur will push you out of your comfort zone, provide rewards, and allow you to grow in a limitless way.

> EMPLOYEE

Get Up Party & Shake a Leg

This will be the best time in your life while you use your brain power to create youe dream business!

CHAPTER 3
CHARACTERISTICS OF THE SUCCESSFUL ENTREPRENEUR

Have you ever thought about what kind of entrepreneur you would be? Do you dream about becoming this successful entrepreneur where everyone knows who you are? Owning a business will require you to develop successful traits that you need in order to make your business a successful story. These character traits will help you chase your dreams with passion and fire so you overcome obstacles. Here are some character traits:

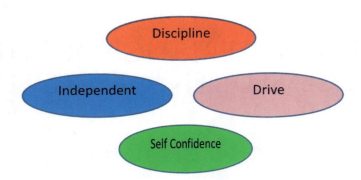

Characteristics Traits of a Entrepreneur

People aren't born with all the necessary character traits needed for success. You must be willing to work at strengthening your character traits by forming great habits and always keep working to make yourself better. Here are a few ways to strengthen your entrepreneurial characteristics:

- You must determine your character strengths.
- Your characteristics must become a habit.
- Develop your characteristic traits that are weak.
- Read articles or books on successful entrepreneurs with great character traits.
- Watch movies about entrepreneurs who overcame obstacles and are achievement oriented.

CHAPTER 4
BUSINESS BLUEPRINT

Starting a business can be a daunting task for anyone to handle. It will take a lot of courage and planning to achieve the results you are looking to accomplish. You are undertaking a journey that can be rewarding if you know the proper steps to take. The business blueprint is a guideline that you can follow to help start the business you always wanted. This step-by-step guide will increase your confidence and build your unique knowledge in business where you will know how to produce a money-making business, as well as sifting through business opportunities. Here are some steps in starting your business:

Use the sections below to write down your ideas, concepts, goals, strategies and research as you plan out your business.

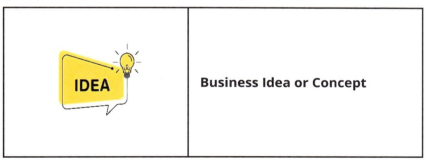

Business Name

- Choose a name that will identify with your brand and make sure its domain is available.
- Make sure your business name is unique and appealing so customers will remember it.
- Check to see if your potential business name is already trademarked or has a similar name trademarked already.

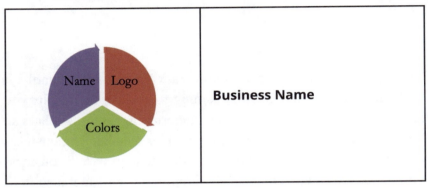

Establish Your Business Goals

- Write your goals down and measure them daily
- Create a specific action plan that is measurable, tangible and realistic for your business to succeed
- Make your goals attainable where you can make it feasible to achieve
- Set deadlines for achieving your goals

	**Business Goals**

Evaluate Your Strengths, Weaknesses, Opportunities, And Threats

- Create a S.W.O.T Analysis to evaluate the pros and cons of your business
- Strategies are formed from the S.W.O.T to make your business a success
- The S.W.O.T Analysis can minimize your weaknesses so you can have an advantage over the competition

Conduct a SWOT analysis. Evaluate Your Strengths, Weaknesses, Opportunities, And Threats

SWAT ANALYSIS	STRENGTHS	WEAKNESSES
	OPPORTUNITIES	THREATS

Determine Start-Up Cost

- The type of business you start will determine the cost you will incur.
- What are your startup expenses?
- Create a spreadsheet that will showcase each monthly expense.
- Remember, you have a pre and post opening costs.
- Always set aside money for unexpected expenses and problems.
- Do you have enough funds to cover expenses until your revenue starts coming in consistently?

THE YOUNG MOGULS

List Start-Up Cost

Evaluate Your Financial Resources

- Do you have a 12-month positive cash flow projection in place?
- Do you have enough cash on hand?
- Do you need to borrow money?
- Are you saving money to start your business?
- Did you look at suppliers as a source of financing?
- Do you have enough working capital to maintain your daily operation?
- How much money can you make in a day, month, year?
- Does that cover your expenses?
- Have you planned out all anticipated expenses or surprises?

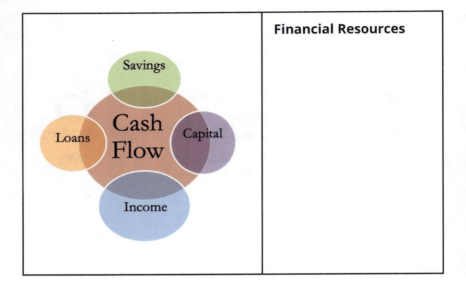

Perform Market Research

You want to gather information about the industry and market you are entering. You must understand your target customer's needs and preferences so you can get the right product out to those who want to purchase your goods or services. Here are some tips:

Determine who your target customers are.

- You must decide what will be the purpose of your study.
- You need to gather data from all resources in order to conduct an accurate market analysis.
- Analyze all the information you have gathered.
- Once your market analysis is completed, now you put it to work. Who is your competition?
- What comparisons do their business and your business share?
- How are you unique?

Perform Market Research

OBTAIN A BUSINESS LICENSE OR PERMIT

- All businesses need to register their name at the city clerk or secretary of state office to receive a business license.
- Is your business zoned for your type of business?
- Do you have a seller permit that allows you to collect sales taxes?
- Do you have a certificate of occupancy?
- What is the cost of the business license?

	**What Kind of Business License or Permit do you Need?**

CHAPTER 5
ENTREPRENEURIAL ASSESSMENT

These days, becoming an entrepreneur will require different types of skills. However, you don't have to go about it in the same way as everyone else. Successful entrepreneurs have multiple personality traits that will determine your strengths and weaknesses.

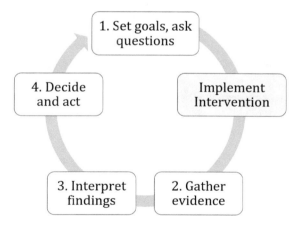

There are simply so many risks to take for such a journey. You will need a strong commitment and specific skills to be a successful entrepreneur. As you assess your characteristics, you will be able to evaluate your best qualities and experiences that will prepare you for this amazing adventure. There aren't any guarantees for success, but if you put in the proper preparation, you can give yourself a chance to create something special with an adequate assessment of your business capabilities.

- How much time are you committed to starting a business?
- Are you creative?
- Do you take risks?
- What is the maximum amount of money you can invest in the business?
- What are your strengths and weaknesses for starting a business?
- Why am I going into business?
- How long do you plan to have your business?
- Are you committed to being the best?

SELF-ASSESSMENT & ONGOING TRAINING

Whatever the reason why you want to start a business, you must identify what skills you have and what areas you need help. You might have to use your own money, possibly go into debt until your business makes a profit. You need to do a self-assessment to provide the first steps in addressing key issues for your business.

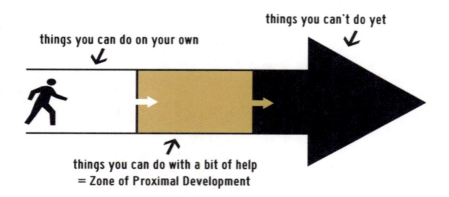

It's critical to evaluate your personal weaknesses along with your strengths. When you identify your weaknesses, you might need to get a partner, manager and extra training to offset your weaknesses. Here are some things to consider before you start your business:

- What skills do you have?
- What experience do you have selling the products and services in your business?
- What experience have you had operating a business?
- Can you recognize and solve problems?
- Will your business be full-time or part-time?
- Do you need training or specialized training?
- What type of products or services will you offer?
- What resources do you have?

Demands of Owning a Business

When you create your business, there will be many things you have to do in order to start it. You will have total control of everything pertaining to the business from the creation, sales, and operation. You will have to make sure everything goes as planned so you give your business the opportunity to survive or just plain flourish in the industry you choose.

Here are some tips:
- Running a business may require you to work 12-18 hours a day, seven days a week.
- If you are blessed enough to make money, do you know how to find good employees?
- Can you make effective decisions?
- Do you have the emotional strength to handle the workload of doing business?

- Will your family be able to handle the pressure of you doing business?
- Do you understand marketing?
- Do you know how to keep good records?
- Do you understand business financing and cash flow management?

Being an entrepreneur requires mental stamina. You will go through a range of emotions, from excitement, fear, stress, anxiety, frustration and anger. Failure is a part of the process to building something new, but SUCCESS can emerge if you do not QUIT during the difficult times.

CHAPTER 6
BUSINESS IDEA

There are many business ideas you can choose from. You must consider what kind of business you want to do. You should dig from your experiences or other sources to come up with what's best for you. Pick from your personal preferences, financial worthiness and risk factors it will take to open a business. I recommend you read articles, books, trade publications and visit existing businesses to give you an idea. Here are some tips:

BE AUTHENTIC

Hobbies

When you look at the history of business, most businesses are started by someone who had a hobby that turned into a profit-making business. Think about how many hours you put into your hobbies where you channeled a beautiful energy because you loved what you were doing. If you put that same love and energy into creating your business from a hobby, you will become a great business owner from the desire and passion you put into it.

Job/Volunteer

Some people who work at a job feel they can improve the business with certain changes. You can provide certain services that are missing, improve on customer relations, and provide a cheaper cost for the customers. The working experience gained can also help you branch out on your own. You can volunteer and gain in-depth experience by learning everything in the business which will help you build your brand. Service can be a form of learning and gaining inside knowledge.

Trade Magazines

Trade magazines publish periodicals of specific businesses. This can give you an idea to research the industry you are looking into. It will give you a wealth of information that you might not have known and help you make a critical decision in picking a certain industry you might want to enter.

Contacts

You can ask people from work, school, church, local organizations, and friends about any opportunities to start a business. You have an abundance of information at your disposal. You just need to create a contact list to make sure you don't leave out any potential resources to help you.

Internet

Many people use the internet to search for various things. The internet can be used to find the hot industries that would help businesspeople choose where customers spend their money. It's a powerful tool that will answer your questions pertaining to creating a business you want or give answers in areas you were unsure about.

CHAPTER 7
LEGAL REQUIREMENTS

When you start a new business, the local government has regulations in place that protect businesses and the public. Laws that protect businesses include patents, copyrights, and trademark laws. The public is protected by regulations that require businesses to be licensed or registered in order to protect consumers from businesses that aren't qualified. Based on the state your business is registered in, you will be required to pay certain fees before you can start your business.

PATENTS

A patent grants the inventor exclusive rights to produce, use and sell an invention for a period of 20 years. In order to receive a patent, you must submit your application to the Federal Patent and Trademark Office (PTO).

Businesses and individuals can't copy or use the patented

invention without the permission from the patent holder. After twenty years, a person may sell your invention without paying the inventor. It takes about two years for a patent to be searched. If the patent already exists, you will be denied the patent. If an invention is in use for more than one year without obtaining a patent, the invention will be considered public domain and will no longer be granted a patent.

COPYRIGHT

A copyright is the legal protection offered to literary, musical and artistic work. You will not be able to sell, print, revise or distribute without the permission from the author.

A copyright lists the publisher and the year it's published. A copyright lasts the life of an author plus seventy years after the death of the author.

TRADEMARK

A trademark is a word, symbol, name, or mark that distinguishes your business or products from those of other businesses. You use the trademark so consumers will recognize your products visually and give your business the marketability edge over the other businesses. A trademark can't be used by anyone else without the permission of the person or business that owns it.

LICENSE

Local governments and state departments require some businesses to have licenses to operate a business. Licensing is used to protect consumers from unskilled and unqualified business owners who can damage or destroy your property. If your business is located within an incorporated city's limits, a license must be obtained from the city, if outside the city limits, then from the county. Often, the issuance of professional or occupational licenses requires the applicant to show certain training or certain skills. In most cases before you open your doors for business, you must get a license to do business in a state. Here are the different types of licenses:

- Federal License (selling alcohol and commercial fishing)
- Local Business License (depends on the city or county of your business)
- State Business License (required for contractors, physicians, accountants and barbers).

PERMIT

You will have to get a permit to start a business in some states. Depending on your business, you may need a building permit to construct a building, health department permit to sell food, and a land use permit to manufacture products. Your permit indicates that you are a professional business. Some states require a regular inspection by state and local authorities to make sure your business is up to par. In some cases, you also must pass exams to show that you have the necessary education and training to do the job. Here are different types of permits:

- Business Permits (basic permits to operate a business).
- Zoning and Land Permits (business signage, specific usage and home-based businesses).
- Building Permits (new building construction and existing building renovations).
- Seller's Permit (selling or leasing goods from a cafe or shop).
- Health Permits (restaurants and food preparation businesses).
- Fire Marshal (department permits and certificates).
- Fictitious Business Name Permit ("DBA") Doing business as an alternative business name.

CHAPTER 8
RECORD KEEPING

One of the biggest mistakes people make when starting a business is keeping poor records. The best way to stay on top of your business is keeping accurate daily records. Good records provide financial data to help you operate your business more efficiently and profitable. It allows you to catch errors before they occur. You will know how much money is coming in and out. Your record-keeping system for a small business might include your business checkbook, daily summary of cash receipts, monthly receipts, and employee compensation records. Basic records you must keep:

General Office Records

Keep documentation for all your business transactions which can be invoices, contracts, purchase orders, and business correspondence in a safe place.

Inventory

Keep track of changes in your inventory. You will investigate items, quantities sold, and what is currently in stock.

Quality Control

Monitor complaints about the quality of your products. Keep track of products that are returned.

Insurance

Keep accurate records of all insurance premiums.

Good Records Will Do the Following:

You want to keep good records because being organized in business is essential in surviving. Some records have a long shelf life where you need to keep them for a long period of time. So, it's very important to know the lifespan of each record you are holding onto. You will be able to separate your personal from your business so you can track all your expenses from income you are bringing in.

Monitor The Progress of Your Business

You need good records to monitor the progress of your business. Records can show if your business is improving or if certain items are selling better than others. Good records will give you the opportunity to increase business success.

You can prepare accurate financial statements by keeping good records. This will include your income statement (profit and loss) and balance sheets. You will be able to manage your business as well as deal with your bank and creditors.

Organize Receipts

You will receive money from different sources.

You will be able to separate business from non-business receipts, and taxable from nontaxable income.

Prepare Your Tax Returns

You need good records to prepare your tax returns. You can record your expenses, credits and income.

Support Items Reported on Tax Returns

Your business records must always be available for inspection by the IRS. You may have to explain certain items on your tax returns. If you have all your receipts available, you will be able to give the IRS exactly what they want.

Gross Receipts

Gross receipts are income you receive from your business. You can use the cash register tapes, bank deposit slips, invoices and credit card slips to get your gross receipts.

Keep Track of Your Expenses

When you are in business, you can forget about all the expenses that are occurring in your business. Forgetting about your expenses could alter your deductions on your tax returns and give you an inaccurate account of your business.

Maintain A Checking Account

One of the first things you should do when you start a business is open a business checking account. Your business checkbook is your basic source of information for recording your business expenses. You should deposit all daily receipts in your business checking account so you can separate your income and loans. Always try to make all payments by check to document all business expenses.

Make Decisions Based on Information Rather Than Guessing

You will know exactly where your business is going with accurate records. You could bankrupt your business by overspending and not properly handling your money with terrible records.

Bookkeeping System

When you start keeping records, you can decide if you want to use a single-entry or double-entry system. A single-entry system is simple to do because it's based on your income statement (profit and loss).

The single-entry system records the flow of your income and expenses through daily summary of cash receipts and disbursements.

You will need to track

Cash Sales--Invoices-Payments-Wages-Expenses

Your double-entry system records your debits and credits which improves the accuracy of your financial statements and detects error's better.

CHAPTER 9
BUSINESS STRUCTURE

Legal Forms of Business

Before you can think about opening your doors for business, you will have to decide what legal form of business you will choose. The legal structure you choose will determine the organization, debt liability, and tax requirements. You have several legal structures to choose that will be the best for your business.

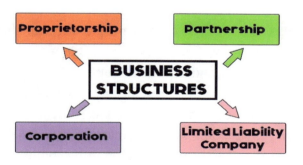

Sole Proprietorship

Sole Proprietorship is the easiest form of business to create, and the simplest form of business organization you can start. The sole proprietor is a business owned by one person. He or she is in total control of all the business aspects and will receive all the business profits or losses. The business liabilities are attached to the owner personally. The owner will take on the risk of all assets, income and expenses on your personal tax returns. The profit or loss of the business is taxed as personal income and is included on the owner's individual tax return.

Before you can become a sole proprietor, you will have to apply for a certificate of doing business (DBA). The DBA is a pseudonym used by businesses that don't operate under their registered company name.

This alternative name is a fictitious business name used to conduct business under a name other than its legal business name.

Partnership

A partnership consists of two or more people who share in the profits and losses of a business. Each person contributes money, property, labor, skills, strengths, and expects to share in the profits and losses of the business. A partnership must file an annual information return to report income, deductions, gains, and losses from its operations, but it doesn't pay income tax. This means they pass through any profits or losses to its partners. Each partner includes his or her share of the partnership items on his or her tax return. Advantages of the partnership:

- You can establish a business with minimal documentation.
- It's the simplest form of business for two or more owners.

- Limited liability partners have a lower risk for losses.
- All partners bring resources and skills to the partnership
- Profits and losses belong to the partners.
- You can have a buy/sell agreement in place.

General Partnership

Each partner will have unlimited personal liability and will have full responsibility for the business. Your general partnership can be formed by an oral agreement between two or more persons.

Each partner will be liable for all debts, taxes and other responsibilities against the partnership. It is required to have at least one general partner where they pledge their personal assets.

Limited Partnership

Limited partners don't have any say in the daily operation of the business. The limited partnership has both general partners and limited partners in the business. They are investors whose liability is the initial investment they put into the business. Limited partners are restricted in the amount of personal liability and don't have any control over management. If a limited partner invests $5,000 in your business, they are only liable to lose the $5,000.

Corporation

A corporation is a legal "person". It's a business that is chartered by a state and legally operates apart from its owners. The corporation is a legal entity that exists under the authority of state law and is separate from the people who own, manage, and control its operations.

There is the C Corporation, S Corporation and Limited Liability Company (LLC.).

The corporation is liable, and the board of directors isn't. The board of directors is a group of people who make major decisions from electing officers, determining salaries, conducting business, and determining how much is paid to shareholders. They also create by-laws and oversee corporate policies.

S CORPORATION

The corporation is set-up to be taxed as a sole proprietor or at the partnership level. Profits are only taxed one time at the shareholder's level. You don't have to pay federal taxes on profits of the corporation. Instead, the IRS allows all profits to pass through to the individual shareholders' personal tax returns. In order to be a S Corporation, it must be a domestic corporation, have no more than 75 shareholders, must have individual estates, certain trust as shareholders, citizens must own stock, and only have one class of stock.

S Corporation is exempt from federal income tax other than taxation on certain capital gains, and passive income where double taxation is avoided. Advantages of the S Corporation:

- Limited Liability.
- Doesn't pay double taxation.
- Owners can be in management.
- You can transfer ownership without restrictions
- Taxed like a sole proprietor or partnership but maintains itself as a corporation.

C Corporation

The C Corporation is set-up to have an unlimited number of shareholders and can have public stock offerings. The corporation is required to pay taxes on the profits and the shareholders are taxed separately from the entity. The taxing of profits from the business is at both corporate and personal levels which create a double taxation situation. The advantages of a C Corporation:

- Limited liability for owners/shareholders.
- You can raise large amounts of capital by issuing stock.
- Continuity of the business beyond original founders or shareholders.
- Separate legal entity.
- Transferability of ownership.

Limited Liability Company (LLC.)

This business structure allows the limited liability company (LLC.) to have the best of both worlds.

An LLC. has the corporate characteristics of the limited liability and the tax advantages plus the flexibility of a partnership. An LLC. is considered a separate entity where you file Articles of Organization with the Secretary of State. Two or more owners must submit the appropriate paperwork.

You are only taxed once at your personal income of the partnership and the use of the corporation protects your personal assets from creditors and lawsuits.

Owners of an LLC. are called members which are comparable to stockholders in a corporation or limited partners in a limited partnership. The LLC. provide for members to contribute money or other considerations to the company where members share in profits and losses plus participate in management. Advantages of an LLC.:

- LLC. is a separate entity.
- None of the members of an LLC. are personally liable for its debts.
- You can have an unlimited number of shareholders.
- Tax benefit is you are taxed on profits at the individual tax rate.
- Various ways you can raise capital.
- Members can be individuals, corporations, partnerships or other LLC.'s.
- You have control over management without risking any liabilities.
- You can transfer membership.

CHAPTER 10
CUSTOMER SERVICE

The first thing you do when you open your business is to offer your customer what they want and not what you want to sell. Customers are always looking for a business that will provide their needs.

Once that customer is satisfied with what you are offering, they will tell their friends, neighbors, and colleagues about your business. You must continue to satisfy your customers in order to maintain their loyalty. By offering a fair price for your products or services in a convenient manner, you will keep your customers coming back.

First Impression

We already know you have one chance to make a first impression. Remember your customers, partners, and employees make decisions on whether to work with you based on your appearance, body language and image. You will not sell anything if you make a bad impression when you meet potential customers. Things to think about with a potential customer:

- Do you leave a clear picture of your business when you talk to potential customers?
- Do you hand out business cards with your contact and social media information?
- Does your appearance fit your business?
- What non-verbal communication do you display?
- Can you take 5 minutes out of your day and practice techniques to enhance your first impression?

Provide Top-Notch Customer Service

Providing top notch customer service will set your business apart from the competition. Remember customer's always shop where they get good value, not necessarily where the best price is offered.

You must treat each customer like royalty because it could be the last time you see them. Business owners lose customers for a variety of reasons. You need to develop a standard that not only meets your expectations but exceeds your customer's expectations.

Here are a few tips:

- Acknowledge your customers as soon as possible.
- Send thank you and holiday cards to your top-notch customers
- Train potential employees to deliver excellent and quality service.
- Reward repeat customers with incentives.
- Reward customers who give referrals.
- Showcase your best customer's input on your website.
- Implement a customer service policy that all members must follow.

Understanding Customer Service

Many people truly don't understand why customer service is so important. We all have been in a place of business and were treated with no respect. Once that experience was over, we vowed to never go back. Most likely the business owner didn't know the customer felt slighted and had a problem shopping at his or her business. Here are some reasons why customer service is so important:

- Dissatisfied customers tell an average of 10 people about their bad experience.
- Satisfied customers will tell their friends and family about your business.
- It will cost your business five times more to attract new customers than keeping existing ones.
- At least 85% of the dissatisfied customers will not buy from you again, and you won't know why.

- Most dissatisfied customers don't complain about poor service.
- The last 30 seconds are critical to establish rapport with a customer.

Strategies To Keep Customers Coming Back

- Create unbeatable products and services.
- Use incentives to keep your customers coming back.
- Believe in your work.
- Show your appreciation to every customer.
- You need to know your top customers and treat them like gold.

- Make your products or services accessible to buy from you instead of your competitors.
- Bring your goods or services to the customer.
- Find out what your customer wants.
- Become a champion in customer service.

CHAPTER 11
SELLING

All business is based on selling goods or services for money. Your business will never get off the ground without being able to sell your idea. In order to become an effective salesperson, you must be enthusiastic about selling, get along with people, know your product, and manage your time wisely. The salesperson's job is to try to figure out how to make a profit. An entrepreneur knows that survival is based on being able to sell their products or services to customers and attract investors for the growth of the business.

Personal Selling

Personal selling is a direct communication between the salesperson and customer. The customer will need personal attention in order to know what they need and if they have any issues. You can use networking techniques, cold calling, or prospecting to sell your products or services to your customers.

Principles of Selling

When you are selling a product or service, you should be listening more than talking. The customer will tell you exactly what they want instead of you trying to sell something. You should remember you technically work for all your customers who are interested in whatever you are offering while you are building a long-term relationship with the customer.

Prospecting

You will have to find potential customers who could benefit from buying your products or services. You can do this by getting the names of prospects from customers who already made purchases from you.

Pre-approach

Gather and analyze information about the prospects buying needs, habits, and price expectations. Getting this information will allow you to better serve your customers and show how you care about their needs.

Approach

You must gain the trust of your customers. You should greet them with a hello. Your main approach is to get an interview so you can make your sales presentation.

Close

You should begin to close a sale after thoroughly presenting the product or service. You must understand when the right time presents itself to close the sale.

Suggestion Selling

After you already closed the sale, suggest additional items your customers could purchase from you. This would introduce your customers to items they haven't seen before which would increase your revenue.

Selling Techniques

Making sales requires you to understand the market you are in as well as build trust with your customers.

You should listen intently with your prospect to understand what they want so you can focus on helping them instead of trying to sell them something.

Always put your customers first and never make the sale about you.

Look Presentable

Make sure you are neat and clean to look presentable. You should be professionally dressed and well groomed. Your customers will judge you based on your appearance and might not do business with you because your image isn't up to par.

Identify Yourself

When you are on the telephone with a customer, always greet them with your name and title. You are trying to develop a relationship with the customer as soon as contact is being made.

The objective is to build a rapport that will last with customers throughout your business relationship.

Have Belief in Your Product

You must believe in your product to become an effective salesperson. Your customer will be able to see through you when you are trying to sell your product and you don't believe it. Remember if you don't truly believe then it will be hard to make someone else believe.

Always Be Prepared

You need to know exactly what your product does. Your customer will ask many questions and you will need to know everything about your product because your customer won't purchase it if you can't explain everything in detail about your product.

Always Think Positive

There will be times when things go wrong. You must always be positive around your customers. Your positive energy will ignite a spark in your customers where they will feel a connection with you that will prompt them to buy from your business.

Build Relationships

You want your customers to come back and buy from you again. You want to grow a customer base that repeat the buying experience with you. Your business will grow faster by catering to the customers you already established a relationship with where your business will grow tremendously by selling multiple products to your repeat customer.

Unique — Sale — Target Audience — Marketing

UNIQUE SELLING POINT

Consumer — Benefits — Difference — Competition

CHAPTER 12
BUSINESS PLAN

Why Is a Business Plan Important?

A business plan is a written document used to help visualize all components of your business and will help get the necessary financing from investors. Your business plan should help you focus on your ideas, create a benchmark for you to measure progress, and help you to track business growth. Your business plan will help bring together your goals, a plan of action, and strategies to help you minimize financial risk.

Your business plan will describe what you will produce, who will manufacture your products and who will be your target customers. Writing a great business plan is of most importance because if your plan isn't all together, the direction of your business will be hard to understand and keep track of. Your business plan should describe:

- Your management team and their experiences.
- Your goals and objectives.
- Your marketing plans.
- Financial statements.
- Business ownership.

What is In Your Business Plan

In order to write a great business plan, you will need to be organized. Your plan should have a cover sheet, table of contents, statement of purpose, executive summary, market plan, financial plan, and appendix. Investors will not want to give you any money because your plan doesn't display an efficient business. Your plan should include the following:

- An introduction describing your business, its goals, and the advantages your business has over the competition.
- Your product description and identifying your competitors in the market.
- A marketing plan shows what products and services you offer. You should identify the customer demands, target marketing, pricing strategy, and advertising you will do.
- You will need financial information including your financial sources, the amount of your initial capital, monthly operating budget, and your return on investment.

Your probability of creating a successful business is based on the accuracy of your business plan.

The preparation you put into it will allow you to put forth a deliberate effort that you can evaluate daily to make sure you are on task, identify the who, what, when, where, how much, and why. Things that go into your business plan:

Cover Sheet

Your business plan cover sheet should have the name of your company, logo, address, date, telephone number, fax number, email address, month and year your plan was completed.

Table Of Contents

A table of contents gives the reader a listing of what is exactly in your business plan. Each section will be aligned together in order to display the accurate information within the business plan.

Statement Of Purpose

Your statement of purpose will be two paragraphs long describing why you need a loan and what you are going to do once you get the loan. You also should explain how long it will take for you to pay back the loan.

Executive Summary

The executive summary is the most important section of your business plan. It should be no longer than two pages and be able to grab the interest of your reader. This will be the first section the investor will see, and you should write this section last after your business plan is completed. You will provide an overview of the entire plan, funds needed, history of the company, management team, financial projections, banking relationships, name of owners, and product plus services you offer.

Market Analysis

The market analysis section should show your knowledge about the industry you are trying to get your business into. This will help you understand your competition. A business owner will find out if an opportunity is available.

Researching the competition, industry, business analysis, will showcase opportunities, strengths, and weaknesses displaying an accurate decision on providing a stellar business model.

Company Description

The company description section should include information about the nature of your business and how it will be a success. You will show how your business satisfies a market need with your product or services plus how your customers will receive it.

Management Plan

This section will include your company organizational structure (management and employee responsibilities), details about ownership, and information about your management team. Your organizational structure will be in a chart form which will show the function of your company, and the legal structure of your business, percentage of ownership, management profiles, resumes of key people, and the names of all the owners.

Marketing Plan

Your marketing plan will describe your marketing strategy. Your advertising strategy, selling techniques, pricing strategy, sales forecast, distribution plan and market penetration strategy will be in your marketing plan. You will ensure your customers know your products or services. Your marketing mix will be in this section breaking down the benefit.s your customers will receive.

Financial Plan

Your financial plan will consist of your company's income statement, balance sheet, profit plus loss statement, and cash flow projections for each year you have been in business (usually 3 to 5 years). Your projections should match your funding request.

Appendix

The appendix section will include any supporting documents pertaining to your business plan. Documents will include:

- Legal forms of ownership
- Credit history
- Licenses, patents, and permits
- Personal financial statements
- Income tax returns
- Contracts
- Letters of reference
- Resumes
- Leases

CHAPTER 13
THE MARKETING MIX

For a business to truly thrive, you will need to put together a marketing plan to showcase your business to potential customers. Your marketing mix will give you a competitive advantage over your competition where your customers will get a better value for their money. The four elements of a marketing program are, planning and developing; pricing the product; placing the product for customers; and promoting the product. Your marketing mix plays an integral role in maintaining and finding customers that help your business thrive.

Product

Once your business is started, you will have to determine what products you will provide for the customers. For your business to survive, the product you are selling must be everything your customers want. You have to offer the right product even if prices are reasonable, some customers will not buy what you are offering. It's very important to understand that by offering what people want they will become loyal to buying your product.

Product Features

The features of your product will include style, color and distinctive characteristics. You want to show the difference between your products compared to your competitors.

Price $$$

Most price markups are based on the price you paid for your product or service plus a percentage of that cost. You must buy low and then sell higher to make a profit. Your prices can be influenced by the number of suppliers, customers and the availability of your product. Most businesses begin a strategy to attract customers if they enter the market with a product lower in pricing than their competitors to appeal to the customer wallet.

How Price Is Affected

Your price can be affected when other businesses in the distribution process go wrong. Each company will add fees to your product that will cause the price to go up which is passed down to the customers. The customer could stop buying the product because the price is too high for them.

Ultimately, the price of your products or services says something about your business where it indicates the quality of your product based on the price.

Promotion

You need your product or service noticed by your potential customers by promoting your business. This will showcase the benefits of buying from you to your customers. You can use it to communicate your message to your customers. Some forms of promotion are coupons, exhibits, tie-ins (two or more companies offering a package deal), and samples.

Place

You will have to determine how you will deliver your product or services. Will you open a location, or will you go to your customers? Whatever you decide, you should make sure your strategy coincides with providing the best option to distribute your products or services. Remember you want your location to be of high quality to make your business standout.

CHAPTER 14
COMPETITION

When you start a business, you need to identify your competitors who are selling the same products as you. For your business to flourish, you must give your customers a reason to ignore the competition and only want to buy from you. You need to make sure your business is better than the competition because customers have a variety of businesses to choose from and receive exactly what is promised to them. Always remember you aren't selling products or services, but you are selling satisfaction to customers who will spend their money on things they like.

DIRECT COMPETITION

When you are selling the same thing as your competitor, you are in direct competition trying to get the same customers. Your competition can be in the same geographic area that provides direct pressure on your business. There is a lot of pressure to distinguish the differences between you and similar businesses.

You must differentiate your business by offering something unique or catchy that will show your differences to the customer.

Indirect Competition

When your competitors offer a different solution to the same target market, they are an indirect competitor. If you are selling hamburgers in a neighborhood and another business is selling hot dogs, then you both are indirectly competing selling food to the same target customer despite you may be selling different products. Most businesses aren't aware that indirect competitors exist, so they don't prepare for those businesses to impact them getting customers and profits. It's very hard to tackle indirect competition because the customer has the decision power in buying exactly what they want despite all your marketing efforts.

Studying Your Competition

You must analyze the strengths and weaknesses of your competition to understand what they are selling. If your business is no better than your competitor, it will be hard for you to succeed due to your potential customers not having a valid reason to try your products or services. You must do a competitive analysis which will show businesses that offer the same thing as you. You will see how many are in your geographic area, what they are offering, prices and the quality of their products or services.

SHAWN SMALLS

Meet the Author

Shawn Smalls, MBA is the CEO of Academic Achievers/S&L Consultants, Co-Founder of The Young Moguls, and Co-Founder of A.C.E. Academy Charter School (K-8), where students learn entrepreneurship and wealth principles. He has spent the last 30 years helping adults and kids start their own small businesses through seminars, lectures, consulting, and workshops.

Made in the USA
Columbia, SC
27 July 2024